instant gratification
cards

instant gratification
cards
FAST & FABULOUS PROJECTS

by Carol Endler Sterbenz and Genevieve A. Sterbenz | Photography by Julie Toy

CHRONICLE BOOKS
SAN FRANCISCO

Library of Congress Cataloging-in-Publication Data:
Sterbenz, Carol Endler.
Instant gratification greeting cards: fast & fabulous projects/by Carol Endler Sterbenz and Genevieve A. Sterbenz;
photography by Julie Toy.
p. cm.—(Instant Gratification)

ISBN 0-8118-2852-2

1. Greeting Cards. I. Sterbenz, Genevieve A. II. Title III. Series.

TT872.S83 2000
745.594' 1—dc21

Printed in Hong Kong

Prop styling by Robin Turk
Designed by Level
Typesetting by Level
The photographer wishes to thank Saadi Howell and Philip Morrison

Distributed in Canada by Raincoast Books
9050 Shaughnessy Street
Vancouver, British Columbia V6P 6E5

10 9 8 7 6 5 4 3 2 1

Chronicle Books LLC
85 Second Street
San Francisco, California 94105

www.chroniclebooks.com

FOR MY DAUGHTER, GENEVIEVE AIMÉE,
who is candlelight on the landscape of my soul.
With love,
MOM

FOR MY MAMA,
Thank you for being such an inspiring and invaluable teacher—
even if on occasion it's cobalt blue.
All my love,
GENEVIEVE

table of

8 Introduction

Chapter 1: Birthdays

12 *The Royal Addition*

14 *Miniature Baby Album*

16 *Peas in a Pod*

18 *Classic Art*

21 *Flirty Purse*

22 *Jeweled Butterfly*

24 *Sweet 16*

contents

Chapter 2: Love

29 *Ransom Note*

30 *Love on the Rocks*

32 *Matchbox Valentine*

34 *Wedding Masterpiece*

36 *Love Knot*

39 *Anniversary Dossier*

40 *Vintage Label*

Chapter 3: Home and Hearth

44 *Bread-and-Butter Notes*

47 *Country Sachet*

48 *Missing Your Easy Company*

50 *Stay in Touch*

53 *Welcome Home*

Chapter 4: Work and Travel

56 *A Room with a View*

59 *Brighter than the Rest*

60 *Fiesta*

62 *On the Road*

65 *Passport*

Chapter 5: Holiday

68 *Paper Lantern*

70 *Christmas Tree*

72 *Festival of Lights*

74 *Coupon Gift Book*

76 *All That Glitters*

78 *Shaken, Not Stirred*

81 *Egg in the Window*

82 *Memory Book*

Chapter 6: General

86 *Center of Attention*

88 *Elegant Note Card*

90 *In the Doghouse*

93 *Sticker Postcard*

94 *Three Little Windows*

96 *Wallpaper*

Envelopes

99 *Gatefold Envelope*

100 *Square Envelope*

101 *Standard Envelope*

102 **Technical Glossary**

104 **Patterns**

108 **Index**

introduction

Greeting cards are one of the most personal ways to convey your sentiments and to connect with family and friends. Although there is a vast selection of cards that you can buy, making a card yourself is simple, and no purchased card will be appreciated more than a handmade greeting. With the instructions in *Instant Gratification: Cards*, you will be able to make great cards in a near instant and commemorate the special events in the lives of those near and dear to you. Organized by occasion, the creative projects on these pages honor birthdays, anniversaries, holidays, friendship, and more.

Our intent with this book is to introduce you to simple techniques that you will be able to use with a variety of interesting materials to create a number of different looks. Armed with these foolproof methods and readily available materials, you will find it easy to create stylish and unique cards for any occasion. A simple T-shirt transfer technique allows you to create charming Bread-

and-Butter Notes (page 44). A dry (inkless) ballpoint pen and a straightedge ruler are all you need to create the elegance of an embossed line associated with fine stationery (page 13). Sheer ribbon transforms into a sachet and slips behind a cutout window in the Country Sachet card (page 47). You'll find many of the materials in your home; the rest are easily purchased at a good craft store. Ribbons, buttons, beads, and glitter always add color or sparkle to any card. Magazines and newspapers contribute ready-to-cut text for the whimsical Ransom Note and Love on the Rocks cards (page 29 and 30). Three simple envelope recipes at the back of the book will help you send your message in style. A handy glossary defines unfamiliar terms.

We truly hope the projects in *Instant Gratification: Cards* will open your eyes to the many creative possibilities. We hope we are able to show you how fun and rewarding it can be to make and give handmade cards to the ones you love.

birthdays

1

12 *The Royal Addition*

14 *Miniature Baby Album*

16 *Peas in a Pod*

18 *Classic Art*

21 *Flirty Purse*

22 *Jeweled Butterfly*

24 *Sweet 16*

The Royal Addition | *finished size: 4¹⁄₁₆″ x 6¼″*

Cut a little window in the front of your card and place a pretty charm that symbolizes the special event within its frame. To add elegance, insert a folio made from paper of different weight and color.

Self-healing mat

Cardstock in white

Lightweight paper

Vellum

Straightedge ruler

Pencil

X-Acto knife

Low-tack masking tape

Dry ballpoint pen

Glue stick

Crown-shaped brass charm, or as desired

Hot-glue gun and glue stick

$1/3$ yard two-sided satin ribbon,

   $3/8$ inch wide

1. On self-healing mat, measure, mark, and cut an $8\frac{1}{8}$-inch-by-$6\frac{1}{4}$-inch rectangle from cardstock, lightweight paper, and vellum, using ruler, pencil, and X-Acto knife.

2. Fold papers in half crosswise. Set vellum aside.

3. On self-healing mat, open lightweight paper flat and lay cardstock over it, right sides facing up, all edges even. Use short lengths of tape at corners to secure.

4. On right panel, draw a $1\frac{1}{8}$-inch-by-$\frac{3}{4}$-inch rectangle on top third of cardstock, using ruler and pencil. Use ruler and X-Acto knife to cut through the double layer of paper along marked lines. Set lightweight paper aside.

5. Turn cardstock to wrong side. Lay ruler $\frac{1}{8}$ inch from cut edge along one side of cutout window. Run dry ballpoint pen along edge of ruler, beginning at one corner and ending at adjacent corner, using pressure to emboss line into cardstock. Repeat to emboss remaining sides, allowing lines to meet at corners. Turn card to right side and use fingers to gently bend edge of frame inward.

6. Use glue stick to glue edge of outside fold of vellum and lay fold on inside fold of lightweight paper, pressing to adhere.

7. Use glue stick to glue edge of outside fold of lightweight paper, then slip into cardstock, aligning folds and pressing to adhere.

8. Lay closed card on work surface and center charm on vellum in cutout window, using a dab of hot-glue to secure.

9. To finish, lay ribbon in center fold like a bookmark.

Miniature Baby Album | *finished size: 3" x 4¼"*

The covers of this miniature album are made luxurious by gluing suede to a paper backing. In an instant, you can create the look of the traditional heirloom baby keepsake. Fill in the pages with information about the new baby and paste in photographs or other ephemera, as desired.

Self-healing mat

Medium-weight paper to match suede

Straightedge ruler

Pencil

X-Acto knife

Kraft paper

Scrap of suede in pastel color

Spray adhesive

Rotary cutter

Patterned white vellum

Stapler and staples

Glue stick

Ribbon

Beads (optional)

Invisible thread and needle (optional)

Note: Always work in a well-ventilated
room when using spray adhesive.

1. On self-healing mat, measure, mark, and cut a 6-inch-by-4¼-inch rectangle from medium-weight paper, using ruler, pencil, and X-Acto knife.

2. Fold liner in half crosswise, creasing center fold with hands, then open flat.

3. Separate two work areas on a flat surface, and cover each with kraft paper. Lay suede wrong side up on one work surface, smoothing suede flat. On the second work surface, open liner flat and lay wrong side up. Spray a light, even coat of adhesive on liner, then lift up and center glue side down on suede, pressing to adhere. Turn suede side facing up to check lamination, making certain suede is flat and smooth against paper. To get rid of wrinkles in suede, peel off suede and reposition.

4. Lay card on self-healing mat, liner side up. Use rotary cutter and ruler to trim suede even with edge of liner paper.

5. If desired, use rotary cutter and ruler to cut bookmark from leftover suede by cutting a 9-inch-long strip ½ inch wide from suede.

6. For pages, measure, mark, and cut two 5¾-inch-by-4¼-inch rectangles from vellum on self-healing mat, using ruler, pencil, and X-Acto knife. Fold pages in half crosswise. Open pages flat and use stapler to secure pages at center fold. Fold folio, then run glue stick along edge of outside fold. Position and press glued fold of folio to inside fold of cover, pressing to adhere.

7. Tie a ribbon around the card. If desired, string beads as pictured on invisible thread and stitch to ribbon before tying.

Peas in a Pod | *finished size: 3" x 3"*

Using ordinary fabric markers and a little square of fabric, you can draw any picture or symbol to commemorate a baby's arrival. Glue it to the center of a small card and it will instantly look like framed art.

YOU WILL NEED:

Self-healing mat

Medium-weight paper in soft yellow

Straightedge ruler

Pencil

X-Acto knife

Scrap of fabric

Scissors

Fabric markers

Fabric glue

1. On self-healing mat, measure, mark, and cut a 3-inch-by-6-inch rectangle from medium-weight paper, using ruler, pencil, and X-Acto knife.

2. Fold in half crosswise, using hands to crease fold. Set aside.

3. Measure, mark, and cut a 1½-inch square of fabric, using pencil, ruler, and scissors.

4. For a ¼-inch fringed edge, pull three or four outside threads on each side of muslin square.

5. In center of muslin, use fabric markers to freehand draw peas in a pod, or use the photograph as a guide.

6. On wrong side of fabric, apply a scant dot of fabric glue to all four corners. Center and press picture on front of card, glue side down.

Classic Art | *finished size:* APPROXIMATELY 5½" x 4¼"

You'll need access to a black-and-white copier to try this nifty printing technique, which substitutes fabulous rag stock paper for ordinary copy paper. In this way you can transfer fine art of any description to cards for every occasion.

YOU WILL NEED:

Self-healing mat

100% rag stock paper

Straightedge ruler

Pencil

X-Acto knife

Copyright-free art: steel-etched engraving,
   or as desired

Note: You will need access to a photocopy
   machine.

1. On self-healing mat, cut an 8½-inch-by-11-inch rectangle from rag stock, using ruler, pencil, and X-Acto knife.

2. Bring art and rag stock to copy center. Test-size art on plain paper, positioning and repositioning art, as well as enlarging or reducing image, as necessary to fit measurements of card. When satisfied with layout, hand feed rag stock into top paper tray following manufacturer's directions. Print copy of art on rag stock, allowing ink to dry completely.

3. Fold printed rag stock in half, then trim away excess paper, as needed.

Flirty Purse | *finished size:* APPROXIMATELY 4½" x 6"

Make a flirty purse in time to wish your best girlfriend "Happy Birthday." Although the card is featured in a reversible patterned paper that you can buy in a stationery store, you can design your own reversible pattern using stationery dots or other self-adhesive stickers on colored paper. Then, you can use it to make one purse and send it off. Or, if you prefer, you can make several purses for your next party and use them as favors.

YOU WILL NEED:

Pencil

Purse pattern (page 107)

Tracing paper

Heavywight reversible paper with pattern

    or cardstock decorated with stickers

    or stationery dots ¼ inch to ½ inch

Lightweight paper in coordinating color

Self-healing mat

Straightedge ruler

X-Acto knife

Glue stick

Adhesive velcro dot

Hot-glue gun

Button or artificial rosebud

Note: You will need access to a photocopy

    machine.

1. Using pencil, trace pattern for purse and folio on tracing paper. Use a copy machine to enlarge pattern. Use pattern as a template to mark on heavyweight and lightweight paper.

2. On self-healing mat, cut out purse and folio sections, using ruler and X-Acto knife.

3. Fold purse and folio sections in half along dash lines. Apply glue to outside edge of folio, then slip inside purse, aligning folds and pressing to adhere.

4. Fold purse in half, bringing top flap over to purse front. Peel the backings from the two-part velcro dot and position dot on back center of flap. Bring flap to purse front and press down, allowing dot to adhere to the front of the purse.

5. Use hot-glue to attach button or rosebud to marked position on front flap.

Jeweled Butterfly | *finished size:* APPROXIMATELY 6" x 3½"

If diamonds are a girl's best friend, this card is sure to please every gal pal on your list. The appeal of the card lies in its shape—a winged butterfly easily cut using an X-Acto knife—and its sparkling jewels.

YOU WILL NEED:

#1 pencil

Pattern (page 106)

Tracing paper

Cardstock in bright color

Dry ballpoint pen

Self-healing mat

X-Acto knife

High-tack glue

Flat-backed rhinestones

1. Using pencil, trace pattern on tracing paper.

2. Lay pattern, wrong side up (penciled side down), on cardstock and use dry ballpoint pen to trace over lines, pressing down firmly to transfer pencil lines. Lift tracing paper from cardstock. The tracing paper will have left a faint penciled pattern on the cardstock.

3. On self-healing mat, cut the butterfly from cardstock using X-Acto knife.

4. Write message as desired on one side of butterfly card and turn card over.

5. Apply glue to underside of largest rhinestones and position as indicated by the pencil lines. Repeat to secure smaller rhinestones.

Sweet 16 | *finished size: 7" x 5"*

The sweet color combinations of this double-layer card can commemorate the birthday of anyone on your list, regardless of age. All you need to do is cut out whatever numerals correspond to the celebrant's age (or the one that flatters him or her) on one piece of colored paper and lay it over a second piece to let a different color show through.

Self-healing mat

**Cardstock in two shades of lemon, one
    solid, one patterned**

Straightedge ruler

Pencil

X-Acto knife

Plain paper

Tracing paper

Number stencils (optional)

Low-tack masking tape

Dry ballpoint pen

Glue stick

Ribbon (optional)

1. On self-healing mat, measure, mark, and cut two 10-inch-by-7-inch rectangles from cardstock papers, using ruler, pencil, and X-Acto knife.

2. Fold cards in half crosswise, laying plain paper over fold and smoothing the crease firmly with clean hands. Set aside.

3. To make a pattern for the age numeral(s), cut a 10-inch-by-7-inch rectangle on tracing paper, folding in half to simulate the card. Open tracing paper flat and freehand sketch desired numeral on the front of the "card," using pencil. If you prefer, you can purchase number stencils at any good craft supply store.

4. Choose one of the cardstock papers to be your outside card. Open this cardstock and lay inside up on your work surface. Turn your pattern over inside up (so that numbers read in reverse) and lay inside the card so that the numerals are on the left panel of card. Make sure all edges are even, and tape corners down to secure. Use dry ballpoint pen to trace each numeral, pressing down firmly to transfer pencil lines. (See Jeweled Butterfly, page 22, step 2.) Remove tape and lift tracing paper from card.

5. On self-healing mat, run blade of X-Acto knife firmly along marked lines of numeral, making sure cuts are smooth. To cut strong curves, hold knife steady and rotate card. For straight lines, use ruler. Remove cutout sections. Open and lay card flat.

6. Use glue stick to apply a line of glue to outside fold of the inside card. Lay this card in the fold of the outside card, pressing to adhere.

7. If desired, center ribbon at inside of fold, bringing ends around to outside of card and tying in a bow.

29 *Ransom Note*

30 *Love on the Rocks*

32 *Matchbox Valentine*

34 *Wedding Masterpiece*

36 *Love Knot*

39 *Anniversary Dossier*

40 *Vintage Label*

love

the
BIRTHDAY
of
my life
Is come,
My love
is come
to me.

C. G. Rossetti

2

Ransom Note | *finished size: 4¾" x 6¾"*

Newspapers and magazines provide letters in beautiful typefaces, ready for you to create any romantic message you care to conjure. Cut and paste them on a card made from overlay film, a shiny paper that will highlight the type and the color of the words you choose.

1. On self-healing mat, measure, mark, and cut a 6¾-inch-by-9½-inch rectangle from cardstock and clear overlay film using ruler, pencil, and X-Acto knife.

2. Lay cardstock and overlay film together, edges even, in vertical position. Fold in half, bringing top edge to meet bottom edge, smoothing crease with hands. Place clear overlay film, wrong side up, on work surface. Set cardstock aside.

3. Cut out letters from newspapers and magazines that pertain to your personal message, using scissors.

4. On back of front panel, use brush to smooth a light coating of decoupage glue over surface of film, spreading evenly. Place cutout letters and ephemera or dried leaves as desired, right side down, on overlay film, using a gentle touch to smooth paper and remove extra glue. Turn overlay film over periodically to check position of words and images. Let glue dry completely.

5. Slip clear overlay film over folded cardstock, all edges even. Center length of ribbon inside fold of card, bringing ends around to outside of card and tying a bow.

Love on the Rocks | *finished size: 6" x 3½"*

Choose just the right words to speak your heart by cutting them out of a magazine and gluing them onto flat-backed glass gems. Your sentiments will suddenly become magnified when you glue them to the front of your card.

YOU WILL NEED:

Self-healing mat

Cardstock in white

Straightedge ruler

Pencil

X-Acto knife

Sheet from newspaper or magazine

Flat-backed glass gems

Scissors

Decoupage glue (such as Modge Podge)

High-tack glue

Note: You will need access to a photocopy machine.

1. On self-healing mat, measure, mark, and cut a 7-inch-by-6-inch rectangle from cardstock, using ruler, pencil, and X-Acto knife.

2. Fold cardstock in half crosswise, smoothing crease with hands. Set aside.

3. Copy words from a newspaper or magazine that expresses your message (such as *I love you*), enlarging selected section as needed using a copy machine.

4. Lay copy on work surface. Place one glass gem on each chosen word of your message and trace around each with pencil. Cut out using scissors. Apply a dab of decoupage glue to the underside of one gem, then position and press down on chosen word so that it can be viewed through top side of gem. Repeat with the remaining words. Position and glue gems to front of card as desired, using high-tack glue to adhere. Let dry.

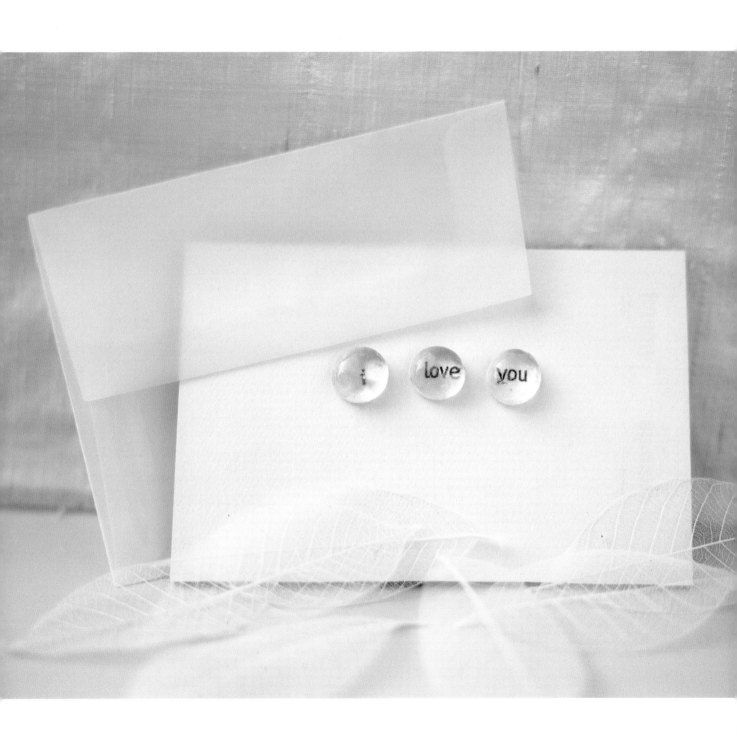

Matchbox Valentine | *finished size:* $1\frac{1}{2}$" x 2" x $\frac{1}{2}$"

If you are set on lighting his fire, decorate a little matchbox with pretty paper and trinkets, and fill the drawer with a scroll-style love letter bound with golden thread.

YOU WILL NEED:

Plain paper

Straightedge ruler

Scissors

Matchbox with drawer

Self-healing mat

Scrap of patterned gift wrap

X-Acto knife

$\frac{3}{8}$ inch-wide ribbon, as desired

High-tack white glue

Ephemera, as desired: trinkets, beads,

   stamps, buttons, etc.

For message scroll: 18-inch length of

   adding machine tape, or plain white

   paper

Ballpoint pen

1. To make a pattern, measure and cut a band from plain paper, using ruler and scissors, that wraps around exterior of closed matchbox, overlapping the ends $\frac{1}{4}$ inch. Test-fit band around matchbox, wrapping snugly.

2. On self-healing mat, lay pattern flat on gift wrap. Use ruler edge and X-Acto knife to trace and cut around pattern. Set aside.

3. Measure and cut a length of ribbon equal in length to band. Lay ribbon on protected work surface. Apply a few dabs of glue to wrong side of ribbon, then glue to center of band, smoothing with hands. Let glue dry.

4. Apply glue to wrong side of band, then neatly reposition around matchbox, as in step #1, smoothing flap down.

5. Add buttons and ephemera, as desired, using a dab of glue to adhere.

6. Trim adding machine tape to 18-inch-by-1$\frac{7}{8}$-inch or measure and cut band from plain paper, using ruler and X-Acto knife.

7. Use pen to write a single sentence across full band of paper.

8. Begin rolling band at end of written text, folding over 3$\frac{3}{8}$ inches to start, continuing to wrap paper around itself until a lozenge-shape scroll forms. Install scroll in drawer, and push drawer shut.

9. Add tassel and tie (see directions below), if desired.

Tassel and Tie (optional)

YOU WILL NEED:

Scrap of chipboard

Straightedge ruler

Pencil

Scissors

Skein metallic gold twine

1. For tassel, measure, mark, and cut a 2$\frac{1}{2}$-inch square of chipboard, using ruler, pencil, and scissors. Wrap metallic twine around chipboard twenty-five times, then cut twine and set aside.

2. To make tie, measure and cut a 5-inch length of twine using ruler and scissors. Thread one end of twine under skein at top of chipboard, pulling twine to midpoint and tying twine in double knot at top of skein and tying the two ends together.

3. Slip blade of scissors between chipboard and skein at bottom of chipboard, cutting through twine.

4. To bind tassel, measure, cut, and wrap a 5-inch length of twine around top of skein, approximately $\frac{5}{8}$ inch below top knot.

5. Use scissors to trim twine even at bottom so that tassel measures approximately 1$\frac{1}{4}$ inches long.

6. Wrap end of gold twine lengthwise around scroll, leaving length 1$\frac{1}{2}$ inches and tassel free. Install scroll in drawer and push drawer shut, allowing $\frac{1}{2}$ inch of twine and tassel to hang from drawer.

Wedding Masterpiece | *finished size: 6" x 6"*

This elegant card suggests that marriage can be a masterpiece. To make a framed reproduction, decorate one square of paper with gold leaf and add an illustration with a creamy white mat.

YOU WILL NEED:

Self-healing mat

Cardstock in cream

Straightedge ruler

Pencil

X-Acto knife

1-ply and 3-ply chipboard

 in white

Rubber cement

Composition gold leaf

Scrap of cream paper

Illustration as desired

Gold paint marker

High-tack glue

Hot-glue gun

1. On self-healing mat, measure, mark, and cut a 12-inch-by-6-inch rectangle from cardstock, using ruler, pencil, and X-Acto knife. Fold in half crosswise. Set aside.

2. Measure and cut a 2¼-inch square of 1-ply white chipboard. Apply a light coat of rubber cement to surface. Lay a sheet of gold leaf on glued surface, tamping leaf in place using a dry finger. Allow to dry overnight.

3. Cut a 1½-inch square of cream paper and a 2-inch square of 3-ply white chipboard. Center and glue cream square to white square using rubber cement.

4. Center and glue a 1⅛-inch-square illustration to cream square using rubber cement.

5. Run gold marker along edge of white chipboard.

6. Glue gilded chipboard to center of front panel of cardstock using high-tack glue. Freehand, cut two ½-inch squares of 3-ply chipboard, gluing them together using hot-glue. Position and hot-glue squares to center of gilded chipboard, followed by framed and matted picture.

Love Knot | *finished size: 3" x 4"*

A simple decorative knot in a field of stark white paper, and two golden rings, focus on two enduring symbols of the marriage ceremony. Although spare, the card is beautiful in its simplicity. The design can also be adapted for use in invitations or in thank-you notes after the wedding celebration.

YOU WILL NEED:

Self-healing mat

Cardstock in white

Straightedge ruler

Pencil

X-Acto knife

5-inch length white cord

Hand-sewing needle

Matching thread

2 silver or golden rings, each 3/4 inch

   in diameter

1. On self-healing mat, measure, mark, and cut a 4-inch-by-6-inch rectangle from cardstock, using ruler, pencil, and X-Acto knife.

2. Lay card in vertical position and fold in half, bringing top edge down to meet bottom edge, and smoothing fold with hands.

3. Tie knot in center of cord, then use threaded needle and thread to sew decorative knot to center front panel of card, making certain stitches do not pull through paper and ending with threaded needle at back of front panel of card.

4. Position the rings against the card below the knot. Stitch to secure.

the
BIRTHDAY
of
my life
Is come,
My love
is come
to me.

C. G. Rossetti

Anniversary Dossier | *finished size:* $4\frac{7}{8}$" x 9"

This creamy white folder can be filled with love letters written on snowy white vellum. The embossed lettering on the cover is a simple and refined touch that signals the importance of the occasion.

YOU WILL NEED:

Self-healing mat

Cardstock in cream

Straightedge ruler

Pencil

X-Acto knife

Rubber stamp with word *Amor*, **or as desired**

Stamp pad in gold, or as desired

Embossing powder in gold, or as desired

Heat gun

Plain vellum

1. On self-healing mat, measure, mark, and cut a $7\frac{1}{2}$-inch-by-$8\frac{3}{4}$-inch rectangle from cardstock, using ruler, pencil, and X-Acto knife. Fold cardstock in half lengthwise, creasing fold.

2. Use rubber stamp and stamp pad to print *Amor* or other word on top third of front right panel. To emboss stamped word, sprinkle embossing powder over wet ink, then gently blow off excess. Use heat gun to melt powder, being careful to move nozzle to avoid overheating powder.

3. To make pages for folio, measure, mark, and cut $3\frac{1}{2}$-inch-by-$8\frac{3}{4}$-inch sheets of plain vellum, using ruler, pencil, and X-Acto knife. Slip folio pages inside cardstock.

Vintage Label | *finished size:* 5½" x 5½"

An often overlooked source of fine illustration is the label on wine and champagne bottles. A pretty label from a special bottle makes a great card and preserves a good memory. You can remove most wine labels by soaking the empty bottle in very hot water for an hour or two, and then coaxing the label off by lifting up one corner. Peel back the label very slowly, allowing hot water to run between the label and the glass bottle. For stubborn glues, you may need to soak the bottle in a large pot of water heated to boiling on the stove. A small drop of detergent added to the water may also help remove the label. Some labels, especially on some imported champagnes, are impossible to remove without tearing. Try a label on a good domestic wine instead. Once removed, pat the label dry and press it between the pages of a heavy book for two or three days.

YOU WILL NEED:

Self-healing mat

Cardstock in cream

Straightedge ruler

Pencil

X-Acto knife

Rubber cement

Label from wine bottle

Cardstock in maroon

1. On self-healing mat, measure, mark, and cut a 5½-inch-by-5½-inch square from cream cardstock, using ruler, pencil, and X-Acto knife.

2. Use rubber cement to affix wine label to center of cream cardstock.

3. On self-healing mat, measure, mark, and cut a 5¾-inch-by-5½-inch rectangle from maroon cardstock, using ruler, pencil, and X-Acto knife. Fold over a ¼-inch-wide flap on left short side, smoothing crease with hands.

4. Lay maroon back panel wrong side up on work surface, flap to the left. Lay decorated front panel on back panel, right edge even. Apply rubber cement to flap and fold over to decorated card front, pressing to adhere. Let glue dry.

44 *Bread-and-Butter Notes*

47 *Country Sachet*

48 *Missing Your Easy Company*

50 *Stay in Touch*

53 *Welcome Home*

home and hearth

3

Bread-and-Butter Notes | *finished size: 5½" x 4¼"*

You'll need access to a photocopy store for this project. Using a heat transfer process used to print T-shirts, you can decorate note cards with any image you want. All you do is color copy the image on special paper and apply the print to your card using an ordinary household iron.

Self-healing mat

Cardstock in ecru

Straightedge ruler

Pencil

X-Acto knife

Medium-weight paper in ecru

Copyright-free art: vintage labels,
** steel-etched engravings, or as desired**

Photo transfer paper

Manicure scissors

Teflon-coated cookie sheet

Household iron

Two $1/2$-yard-lengths satin ribbon,
** $1/8$ inch wide**

1. On self-healing mat, measure, mark, and cut a $5\frac{1}{2}$-inch-by-$8\frac{1}{2}$-inch rectangle from cardstock, using ruler, pencil, and X-Acto knife.

2. Repeat step 1 using medium-weight paper.

3. Lay cardstock vertically on work surface and fold in half crosswise, smoothing folds. Repeat with liner.

4. Bring art and photo transfer paper to copy store, along with pre-cut papers. Use a black-and-white copier to test-size chosen art, enlarging or reducing art to fit front panel of cardstock.

5. Use color copier to copy *mirror image* of art onto transfer paper, following manufacturer's directions.

6. Use manicure scissors to trim image to within $\frac{1}{4}$ inch of outline.

7. Lay card flat, right side up, on cookie sheet. Empty iron of any water and preheat to highest setting, making certain steam feature is turned off. Center transfer art on front panel, wrong side up.

8. Press iron lightly on back of transfer paper to set up adhesion, constantly moving iron to avoid burning paper. Press edges and all sections, then lift up one corner and peel off backing completely. To aid peeling process, use blade of knife laid flat on paper to lift any resistant section of transfer paper. Caution: Reheat any area where paper does not lift easily. Do not iron over printed illustration—it will smear. Let illustration cool.

9. Refold cardstock and position folded medium-weight paper inside, aligning folds. Center ribbons at inside fold of folio, bringing ends around to outside of card and tying ribbon in bow.

Country Sachet | *finished size: 5½" x 4¼"*

This sweet little card doubles as a drawer sachet. Made from sheer ribbon, the sachet is slipped between the front panels of a French fold card with a cutout window. After the card bears its good greeting, it can be slipped between the luxurious folds of lingerie or fluffy towels.

YOU WILL NEED:

Cardstock in pale pastel

Self-healing mat

Straightedge ruler

Pencil

X-Acto knife

8½-inch length of sheer ribbon,
  3 inches wide

Sewing machine or sewing needle

Cotton thread

1 package rose and lavender potpourri,
  or other scent as desired

Clear cellophane tape

Colored marking pens

1. Lay an 8½-inch-by-11-inch rectangle of cardstock in horizontal position on a flat work surface.

2. Fold cardstock in half lengthwise, bringing top edge down to meet bottom edge, smoothing fold with hands. Fold in half widthwise, bringing left edge over to meet right edge, smoothing fold with hands. Unfold second fold so rectangle is horizontal, and lay on self-healing mat.

3. Measure, mark, and cut a 2⅞-inch-by-1⅞-inch rectangle on center of right panel, using ruler, pencil, and X-Acto knife, being certain to cut through both layers of cardstock while holding firmly to prevent stock from shifting.

4. Fold an 8½-inch length of ribbon in half, using sewing machine or needle and thread to stitch two long sides and bottom fold ¼ inch from edge. Sprinkle approximately 1 teaspoon of potpourri into bag, distributing material evenly. Stitch ribbon closed ¼ inch from raw edge.

5. Open fold and center sachet over window, taping sides to secure. Refold card and stitch border around cutout window, ⅜ inch from cut edge. To finish, hand inscribe names of elements in potpourri around window border using colored marking pens, as desired.

Missing Your Easy Company | *finished size: 4¼" x 6¼"*

This card will remind your friends that they are missed. Taking only minutes to make, the cover is embossed with a symbol of comfort, an easy chair. The inside folio is designed to hold little packets of photographs, while a silk ribbon binding holds the sentimental memento together.

YOU WILL NEED:

Self-healing mat

Cardstock in soft green

Straightedge ruler

Pencil

X-Acto knife

Rubber stamp with 1-inch-high image of
  an easy chair, or as desired

Stamp pad in dark green

Embossing powder in dark green

Soft-bristle paintbrush

Heat gun

2 photographs

½ yard silk variegated ribbon,
  ⅛ inch wide

1. On self-healing mat, measure, mark, and cut cardstock into a 12¼-inch-by-6¼-inch rectangle, using ruler, pencil, and X-Acto knife.

2. Fold in half crosswise, smoothing crease with hands.

3. Open card flat, inside fold facing up. Fold 2¼-inch flaps of cardstock toward center fold.

4. Close card so that front right panel faces up.

5. Press stamp in pad and print one image on top third of card. Sprinkle embossing powder on wet ink, gently blowing away excess or using a soft brush to remove stray particles. Melt powder using heat gun, being careful to move nozzle to avoid overheating.

6. Fill card with photographs. Close and secure with ribbons.

Stay in Touch | *finished size: 4" x 5½" x ½"*

Before you bid good-bye to your neighbors or friends on their moving day, slip this stout card filled with ready-to-send envelopes and note cards into their hands. Secured by their flaps with a satin cord or gold elastic cord stretched around the spine, each envelope is already stamped and ready to send. Staying in touch will be suddenly very easy.

YOU WILL NEED:

Self-healing mat

Cardstock in white

Straightedge ruler

Pencil

X-Acto knife

Dry ballpoint pen

Beads: 18–20 brightly colored seed beads;
   bead ½-cm diameter (optional)

"T"-pin (optional)

Sewing thread (optional)

Needles: darning and fine sewing
   (optional)

Two-hole button, ½-inch diameter
   (optional)

String (optional)

6 notecards with matching envelopes in
   coordinated color, or as desired

6 postage stamps

2 yards satin cord or elastic cord

1. On self-healing mat, measure, mark, and cut an 8½-inch-by-5½-inch rectangle from cardstock, using ruler, pencil, and X-Acto knife.

2. Lay cardstock flat in a horizontal position. Measure and lightly draw two vertical lines, each 4 inches from outside edges of cardstock, using ruler and pencil.

3. Lay cardstock flat and run dry ballpoint pen against ruler, pressing down firmly on cardstock to score vertical lines.

4. Use hands to crease scores to form a ½-inch-wide spine.

5. If desired, decorate spine with beads. Use "T"-pin to puncture starter holes along center of spine, each approximately ¼ inch apart. Thread sewing needle and push needle up from inside spine ¼ inch from one edge, exiting at outside of spine. Slip one seed bead onto needle and reinsert needle in exit hole to secure bead. Repeat until all beads are affixed to spine, ending thread in a double knot at inside spine at opposite side.

6. If desired, make button and bead closure. Lay cover flat, wrong side up, then mark midpoint of inside right panel, ¼ inch from edge. Make starter hole by inserting "T"-pin through panel at marked point. Double knot one end of string and thread opposite end through darning needle and insert in hole, exiting at

outside right panel. Slip a fat bead onto needle and secure bead at end of string with a double knot. Attach button by marking the midpoint of left inside panel, ¼ inch from edge. Make starter hole by inserting "T"-pin through panel at marked point. Double knot one end of string, thread through sewing needle and insert in hole, exiting at outside left panel. Insert needle in button and secure button to cover with several

stitches. Close card and wrap beaded string around button.

7. Put one notecard in each envelope and affix stamp as appropriate. Set aside.

8. Stretch length of satin cord or elastic around spine of card and tie ends until elastic is snug enough to hold envelopes, adding bands as needed.

9. Position flaps under elastic at inside spine, flaps facing left inside panel.

Welcome Home | *finished size: 8¼" x 3¾"*

You can combine great swatches of color and neat letters by pairing color samples from paint companies with self-adhesive letters you peel off a backing sheet. Paste some squares in a tumbling line and add any message you want.

YOU WILL NEED:

Self-healing mat

Medium-weight paper in cream

Straightedge ruler

Pencil

X-Acto knife

5 paint chips from paint manufacturer

High-tack glue

Press type

Two 4¼-inch lengths 1½-inch-wide ribbon

1. On self-healing mat, measure, mark, and cut two rectangles, one 8¼ inch by 3¼ inch and one 16½ inch by 3¾ inch, each from medium-weight paper, using ruler, pencil, and X-Acto knife.

2. Fold larger rectangle in half crosswise, then open flat with front right panel facing up.

3. To prepare paint chips, use ruler and knife to trim each sample so that it measures approximately 1 inch square, cutting off manufacturer's text.

4. Position and glue each square across front right panel of card as desired, using high-tack glue to secure.

5. Peel individual adhesive letters from paper backing and press in place on color square, arranging letters of word *welcome* as shown, or as desired.

6. Position and glue one length of ribbon to left front side of card, aligning left edge of ribbon with edge of fold. Repeat, gluing length of ribbon to right side of page, edges even. Overlap and glue ribbon edges to wrong side of front panel, then conceal with 8¼-inch-by-3¼-inch panel.

4

work and travel

56 *A Room with a View*

59 *Brighter than the Rest*

60 *Fiesta*

62 *On the Road*

65 *Passport*

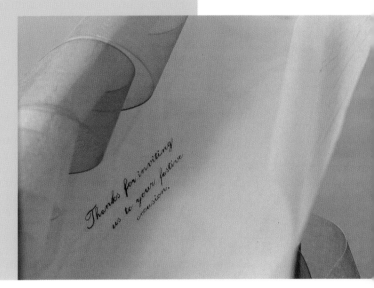

A Room with a View | *finished size: 8½" x 6½"*

Here is an inexpensive and beautiful way to share your trip with a friend. Simply cut up a post-card in sections that replicate the view from behind a mullion window, like that found on a French door, and instantly create the impression that you are actually looking over the scene.

YOU WILL NEED:

Self-healing mat

Cardstock in grey

Straightedge ruler

Pencil

X-Acto knife

Postcard of a black-and-white photograph
    showing a landscape or cityscape

Black marker

Rubber cement

1. On self-healing mat, measure, mark, and cut a 13-inch-by-8½-inch rectangle from cardstock using ruler, pencil, and X-Acto knife, then fold in half crosswise.

2. Place postcard face down on self-healing mat and measure, mark, and cut nine sections to simulate the panes on a window.

3. Use marker to blacken cut edges of each section.

4. Turn postcard sections to right side.

5. Glue postcard pieces to front of card configuring pieces like the panes of a window.

Brighter than the Rest | *finished size: 7" x 5"*

What better way to acknowledge a coworker, employee, or boss than to send a card saying what a fabulous job that person is doing! The graphic beauty of this card is dependent upon the layering of papers with different textures and colors.

YOU WILL NEED:

Self-healing mat

Cardstock in blue and yellow

Straightedge ruler

Pencil

X-Acto knife

Corrugated paper in white

Stencil with sun motif

High-tack glue

1. On self-healing mat, measure, mark, and cut a 10-inch-by-7-inch rectangle from blue cardstock using ruler, pencil, and X-Acto knife.

2. Lay cardstock vertically on a work surface and fold in half crosswise, smoothing folds. Set aside.

3. On self-healing mat, measure, mark, and cut a $3\frac{1}{2}$-inch-by-$3\frac{1}{2}$-inch square from corrugated paper, using ruler, pencil, and X-Acto knife. Set aside.

4. Lay stencil on yellow cardstock and use pencil to trace. On self-healing mat, cut out sun, using X-Acto knife.

5. Place card vertically on work surface and glue sun to center of corrugated paper, then glue corrugated paper to center of cardstock.

Fiesta | *finished size: 8½″ x 11″*

Made from snippets of ribbon, a top border of colorful flags can greet the recipient of this card. Cut 1-inch to 3-inch strips of ribbon in varying widths and don't worry about the raw edges; they lend to the casual feel of this card. After you have inscribed your message, simply roll the card into a scroll and insert it in a mailing tube along with a packet of confetti.

YOU WILL NEED:

Self-healing mat

Cardstock or decorative paper in white

Straightedge ruler

Pencil

X-Acto knife

Sheer ribbon in jewel tones

Scissors

Glue stick

**Mailing tube 1½ inches in diameter,
10 inches long (optional)**

Confetti (optional)

1. On self-healing mat, measure, mark, and cut a 9-inch-by-12-inch rectangle from cardstock, using ruler, pencil, and X-Acto knife.

2. Cut ribbon in varying lengths and widths, using scissors.

3. Lay ribbons in line across top of cardstock, allowing ends to overlap edge.

4. Use glue stick to secure ends of ribbon to cardstock.

5. Fold top of cardstock over glued ribbon ends to create a 1-inch-wide flap. Secure flap with glue.

6. If desired, roll and insert the card into the mailing tube, along with confetti.

Thanks for inviting us to your festive occasion.

On the Road | *finished size: 7" x 5½"*

Ephemera is a great source for fabulous art to decorate your cards. Pretty stamps, cigar bands, and theater tickets can be combined with other items of varying sizes, shapes, and colors to create a kind of sentimental time capsule.

YOU WILL NEED:

Self-healing mat

100% rag stock in ecru

Medium-weight paper in ecru

Gift wrap with postal motifs

Straightedge ruler

Pencil

X-Acto knife

Ephemera: canceled stamps, twine, brown kraft paper, stickers, dried foliage, brass charms, vintage newspaper, or other items

Hot-glue gun

High-tack white glue

1. On self-healing mat, measure, mark, and cut three 14-inch-by-5½-inch rectangles from rag stock, medium-weight, and gift wrap papers, using ruler, pencil, and X-Acto knife. Fold rag stock in half crosswise, smoothing fold with hand. Repeat for remaining papers.

2. Open rag stock card flat, right front panel facing up.

3. Arrange chosen ephemera in a random cluster on right panel, moving elements until satisfied with composition.

4. Secure elements as follows: beginning with background, carefully pick up one item at a time, using a scant dab of hot-glue (for heavier or nonporous objects) or white glue (for lightweight porous objects), securing items to card or to one another. Glue remaining layers of decorative elements, working out to top layer, securing each object with glue.

5. Stack remaining papers, aligning folds.

6. Slip folio into folded card.

Passport | *finished size: 3½" x 5"*

You'll be inspired to pack your bags by the time you finish this charming replica of an official passport. Enhancing the effect is stamped embossing with the image of your choosing. You can find embossing stamps at craft and stationery stores. Alternatively, you can use an adhesive seal.

YOU WILL NEED:

Pencil

Straightedge ruler

Pattern (page 106)

Plain white paper

Self-healing mat

X-Acto knife

Scissors

Medium-weight paper in green or blue

Stationery in coordinating color

Stapler

Embossing tool

Self-adhesive seal

1. Using pencil and ruler, trace pattern for cover and folio on plain white paper.

2. On self-healing mat, use ruler and X-Acto knife to cut out pattern, using scissors to cut around curves, if necessary.

3. On self-healing mat, lay pattern flat on medium-weight paper. Trace and cut out cover, using pencil, ruler, X-Acto knife, and scissors.

4. Use pattern to cut out three inside folios from stationery, as in step 3. Fold papers in half crosswise. Slip folio inside cover section, aligning folds.

5. Open flat and use stapler to secure papers, affixing one staple at top and bottom of fold, each 1 inch from edge.

6. Insert the front cover into the embossing tool, bottom end first. Center the embosser on the bottom third of the cover. Press to emboss. Or, remove seal from adhesive backing and position on front cover, centering it on the bottom third of front panel.

68 *Paper Lantern*

70 *Christmas Tree*

72 *Festival of Lights*

74 *Coupon Gift Book*

76 *All That Glitters*

78 *Shaken, Not Stirred*

81 *Egg in the Window*

82 *Memory Book*

holiday

5

Paper Lantern | *finished size:* 3″-DIAMETER COLLAR SHAPE, 3″ HIGH

This holiday card doubles as a lantern when you shape it into a collar and slip it over a glass votive with lighted candle. The lantern's window, made from frosty vellum and stamped with a holiday motif, emits a warm glow when the candlelight shines through. Add a sprinkling of stars using a paper punch.

Self-healing mat

Cardstock in green

Lightweight paper in metallic gold

Straightedge ruler

Pencil

X-Acto knife

Vellum

Cellophane tape

Coarse-bristle paintbrush

High-tack white glue

Rubber stamp with holiday motif: angel,
   tree, holly leaf, cherub, or as desired

Stamp pad in gold

Embossing powder in gold (optional)

Heat gun (optional)

Hole punch with star motif

Self-adhesive sticker in star motif, or as
   desired

1. On self-healing mat, measure, mark, and cut two 12-inch-by-3-inch rectangles, one from cardstock and one from lightweight paper, using ruler, pencil, and X-Acto knife.

2. Cut a 3-inch-by-2$\frac{1}{2}$-inch rectangle from vellum. Set aside. Lay cardstock and lightweight paper together, all edges even. Measure and cut a 2$\frac{1}{2}$-inch-by-2-inch window in center of card, using ruler and X-Acto knife, cutting through both papers. See diagram. Set lightweight paper aside.

3. Lay card wrong side up on a flat work surface. Center vellum over cutout window, taping to secure.

4. Brush a very light film of glue on wrong side of cardstock. Lay lightweight paper over glued cardstock, all edges even, and smooth flat using hands.

5. Lay card flat in horizontal position, right side up, and use rubber stamp and pad to print a holiday image in center of vellum window.

6. If desired, emboss the card using embossing powder and heat gun. See step 2 of the Anniversary Dossier on page 39.

7. To finish, use hole punch to cut stars into card. Send flat and enclose sticker. To form lantern, shape card into a cylinder, overlapping card at back. Use star sticker to secure.

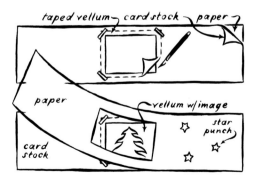

Christmas Tree | *finished size: 5" x 8½"*

You can make your own pop-out greeting cards using oversized rubber stamps. After you stamp your motif over a center fold, cut along the contour of one part of the image and that portion will pop out when you open the card.

YOU WILL NEED:

Self-healing mat

Cardstock in white

Straightedge ruler

Pencil

X-Acto knife

Rubber stamp with 3½-inch-high pine

    tree motif

Stamp pad in green

Embossing powder in clear

Soft-bristle brush

Heat gun

Manicure scissors

Calligraphy pen

1. On self-healing mat, measure, mark, and cut an 8½-inch-by-11-inch rectangle from cardstock, using ruler, pencil, and X-Acto knife.

2. Fold card as shown in picture. Unfold and lay flat.

3. Press tree stamp onto ink pad so that rubber surface is completely covered. Center image, ink side down, along the center fold of left panel, pressing to transfer motif. Sprinkle clear embossing powder over stamped image, shaking paper to remove excess powder and using soft brush to remove any stray particles. Place heat gun over stamped area until embossing powder melts.

4. Use manicure scissors to cut around right side of tree, following stamped contours. Repeat step 3 as desired, centering stamp along center fold of card, and left and right edges as pictured.

5. Use X-Acto knife and ruler to mark and cut two bands as indicated in photo.

6. Use calligraphy pen to handwrite "Joy To The World," or desired message, on bands as indicated in photo.

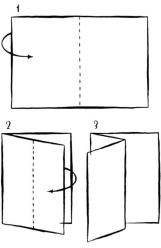

Festival of Lights | *finished size: 6" x 6"*

Create this beautiful Hanukkah card from simple materials like gift wrap and charms to celebrate the traditions of the holiday season. Any cardstock can be transformed by laminating the gift wrap onto the background paper and adding a decorative accent.

Kraft paper

Self-healing mat

Cardstock

Straightedge ruler

Pencil

X-Acto knife

Gift wrap in lavender and white

Scissors

Spray adhesive

Deckling scissors

Menorah or Star of David charm

Hot-glue gun

Note: Always work in a well-ventilated

room when using spray adhesive.

1. Separate two work areas on a flat surface, and cover each with kraft paper.

2. On self-healing mat, measure, mark, and cut a 6-inch-by-12-inch rectangle from cardstock, using ruler, pencil, and X-Acto knife.

3. Lay cardstock flat in horiontal position and fold in half, bringing left edge to meet right edge, smoothing fold with hands. Set aside.

4. Cut roughly an 8-inch-by-14-inch rectangle from lavender gift wrap using scissors.

5. Lay gift wrap wrong side up on one work surface, smoothing flat with hands. On second work surface, open card flat and lay right side up. On card, spray a light, even coat of adhesive, then lift and center glue side down on gift wrap, pressing to adhere. Turn card gift wrap side up to check lamination, making certain wrap is flat and smooth against cardstock.

6. Lay laminated paper on self-healing mat, card side up. Use ruler and X-Acto knife to trim gift wrap even with edge of card.

7. Fold card in half.

8. Cut a 2-inch square of white gift wrap using deckling scissors. Place upside down on work surface and spray a light coat of adhesive. Lift and center square, glue side down on card, pressing to adhere.

9. Glue menorah or Star of David charm to center of white gift wrap, using hot-glue gun to adhere.

Coupon Gift Book | *finished size: 4" x 6" x ¼"*

The secret of this card's appeal lies in the perforated pages made by machine stitching without thread. The row of tiny holes allows you to create coupons you can tear out. Now you can give gifts that would never fit in any gift box—a night on the town, a favorite meal, or a back rub.

Pattern (page 107)

YOU WILL NEED:

Pencil

Straightedge ruler

Pattern (page 107)

Plain white paper

Self-healing mat

X-Acto knife

Medium-weight paper in white with semi-
   gloss finish

Copyright-free art: full-color illustrations
   with holiday motifs, or as desired (e.g.,
   vintage labels, maps, photographs)

Dry ballpoint pen

Sewing machine or "T"-pin

Pad white paper, 4-inch-by-6-inch,
   ¼-inch thick

Contact cement

Wooden cutting board

Staple gun and staples

Colored markers

Self-adhesive stickers

1. Using pencil and ruler, trace pattern on plain white paper.

2. On self-healing mat, cut an 8½-inch-by-11-inch rectangle from medium-weight paper, using ruler, pencil, and X-Acto knife.

3. Bring paper, chosen full-color art, and pattern to copy store. Use a black-and-white copy machine to enlarge and make several copies of pattern. Lay copied patterns, print side up, in top paper tray or follow manufacturer's directions, then position art face down on glass of copy machine. Test-size art, enlarging or reducing image as necessary to fit measurements of front panel of matchbook pattern.

4. When satisfied with layout, use a color copier to hand feed medium-weight paper into paper tray, following manufacturer's directions. Print copy of art, allowing ink on copy to dry completely.

5. Fold printed paper according to dash lines on pattern, scoring lines for easy folding using ruler and dry ballpoint pen. Set aside.

6. Use sewing machine without thread to sew a line of perforations across all pages of the pad, five to eight pages at a time, 1¼ inches above edge of paper at glued end, or use "T"-pin to puncture holes in straight lines.

7. Brush cement on spine of pad and inside fold of bottom flap of

Note: You will need access to a photocopy machine.

matchbook, then wait four minutes, or until cement is tacky. Stand glued spine of pad in glued inside fold of matchbook, pressing down to adhere. Crease score lines using hands so that they hug spine of pad.

8. Place matchbook on a wooden cutting board, bottom flap up. Position nose of staple gun on center of flap and squeeze trigger to affix staple.

9. Use your imagination to write duplicate personal messages on each page, using markers, stickers, and free-hand drawings as desired to set up coupon-style layout.

10. Fold over top flap of cover, tucking bottom edge behind front bottom flap.

All That Glitters | *finished size:* 8¼″ x 5¾″

Everyone loves things that sparkle and shine at holiday time. This card lets you use postcards in a new and exciting way by highlighting certain parts with all the bright and vivid colored glitter available today.

YOU WILL NEED:

Self-healing mat

Cardstock in cream

Pencil

Straightedge ruler

X-Acto knife

Postcard with snowflake design

Fine-bristle paintbrush

High-tack glue

Glitter in coordinating color

Rubber cement

1. On self-healing mat, measure, mark, and cut an 8¼-inch-by-11½-inch rectangle from cardstock using pencil, ruler, and X-Acto knife.

2. Lay cardstock flat in vertical position and fold in half, bringing top edge to meet bottom edge, smoothing fold with hands. Set aside.

3. Lay postcard on a flat work surface and use paintbrush to apply high-tack glue to desired areas, followed by glitter in coordinating color.

4. Repeat step 3 to add glitter details, as desired.

5. Trim postcard as desired, using ruler and X-Acto knife.

6. Use rubber cement to affix postcard to center front of folded cardstock, allowing glue to dry.

Shaken, Not Stirred | *finished size: 5" x 7"*

What better way to ring in the New Year than to keep in touch with friends and family by sending them a card of good cheer? This sleek and modern card is decorated with cutouts of martini glasses that overlap like a double exposure. A plump olive with a real toothpick decorates the inside panel.

Self-healing mat

Vellum

Straightedge ruler

#1 pencil

X-Acto knife

Pattern (page 104)

Tracing paper

Lightweight paper in metallic silver

Dry ballpoint pen

Rubber cement

Scissors

Scrap cardstock in green

Nail polish in glossy red

"T"-pin

Toothpick

1. On self-healing mat, measure, mark, and cut a 5-inch-by-7-inch rectangle from vellum using ruler, pencil, and X-Acto knife. Set aside.

2. On self-healing mat, measure, mark, and cut a 10-inch-by-7-inch rectangle from vellum using ruler, pencil, and X-Acto knife.

3. Fold cover in half crosswise, using hands to crease fold. Set aside.

4. Using pencil and ruler, if necessary, trace martini glass pattern onto tracing paper.

5. Lay pattern, wrong side up, on wrong side of silver paper. Use pen to transfer pencil lines, pressing down firmly. (See Jeweled Butterfly, page 22, step 2.) Repeat on wrong side of grey paper.

6. On self-healing mat, cut out the silver and the grey martini glasses, using X-Acto knife and ruler.

7. Lay folded card right side up on work surface. Apply rubber cement to wrong side of grey glass and press to card glue side down, as pictured. Repeat to position and press silver glass to card front, as pictured.

8. Use pattern and scissors to mark and cut olive shape from green paper.

9. Use nail polish to paint red dot on olive shape.

10. Use "T"-pin to make starter holes in pimiento at marked positions. Insert one end of toothpick in hole in pimiento, pushing toothpick out through second hole.

11. Open card flat on work surface, inside up. Apply rubber cement to wrong side of olive and press to bottom right corner of right inside panel.

12. Write a message on the 5-inch-by-7-inch vellum rectangle and slip into card.

Egg in the Window | *finished size: 3½″ x 3½″*

This sweet Easter card is a perfect accent for a beautiful bouquet of flowers or a chocolate bunny. The card is made simply by applying glitter in an egg shape to the inside panel and by cutting out an egg shape from the front panel of the card so the sparkle shows through.

YOU WILL NEED:

Self-healing mat

Cardstock in pale yellow

Straightedge ruler

#1 pencil

X-Acto knife

Pattern (page 105)

Tracing paper

Dry ballpoint pen

Fine-bristle paintbrush

High-tack glue

Micro-glitter in pastel color

Ribbon (optional)

1. On self-healing mat, measure, mark, and cut a 3½-inch-by-7-inch rectangle from yellow cardstock using ruler, pencil, and X-Acto knife.

2. Lay cardstock flat in vertical position and fold in half, bringing top edge to meet bottom edge, smoothing fold with hands. Set aside.

3. Using pencil, trace egg pattern on tracing paper.

4. Open card and lay in vertical position, wrong side up.

5. Center pattern, wrong side up, on top half of card and use pen to transfer pencil lines, pressing down firmly. (See Jeweled Butterfly page 22, step 2.) Lift off tracing paper.

6. On self-healing mat, cut out oval shape along marked line, using X-Acto knife. Close card. Using pencil, lightly trace along inside of egg shape. Open card.

7. Dip paintbrush in high-tack glue and cover surface area of traced egg. Sprinkle glitter over glued area, shaking off excess. Let glue dry.

8. If desired, add ribbon trimming. Glue a section of ribbon to glittered egg, or a ribbon bow to front cover.

Memory Book | *finished size: 4½" x 6"*

This romantic book is made by sewing folios of translucent papers into a sentimental keepsake. Whatever personal messages, drawings or poems are inscribed on the layers of vellum, all can be seen in a collision of line and color.

YOU WILL NEED:

Self-healing mat

Vellum

Straightedge ruler

Pencil

X-Acto knife

Fine sewing needle

Cotton thread in lavender

Sewing machine (optional)

T-pin (optional)

High-tack white glue

Dried flower or floral sticker

1. On self-healing mat, measure, mark, and cut six 9-inch-by-6-inch rectangles from vellum, using ruler, pencil, and X-Acto knife. Choose two as cover, and set others aside.

2. Lay cover rectangles together, all edges even. Fold cover in half crosswise, using hands to crease fold.

3. Lightly sketch a 1½-inch rectangle on front of cover, using pencil and ruler. Open cover and lay flat on work surface, right side up. Cut out rectangle, using ruler and X-Acto knife.

4. Whipstitch around the edge of window using needle and thread. Whipstitch two cover sheets together around all four sides.

5. Fold remaining pages of vellum in half crosswise, using hands to crease fold. Open folio flat to wrong side and stitch center fold, using a straight stitch or sewing machine.

6. Lay cover flat on work surface, wrong side up. Lay folio flat on cover, wrong side up, aligning folds. Stitch along fold, stitching through cover and folio, using a straight stitch. Use T-pin, if necessary, to puncture holes to aid stitching.

7. Lay card flat on work surface. Glue dried flower to first page of folio, or apply floral sticker, centering flower in the cutout window.

general

86 *Center of Attention*

88 *Elegant Note Card*

90 *In the Doghouse*

93 *Sticker Postcard*

94 *Three Little Windows*

96 *Wallpaper*

Center of Attention | *finished size: 5" x 7"*

The debossed line that forms the square on the front panel of this card is made by pressing a dry ballpoint pen against the edge of a ruler. The line, indented ever so slightly, frames the delicate accent placed therein. The deckled edge is made by tearing paper against the edge of the ruler and furthers its elegant understatement.

YOU WILL NEED:

Straightedge ruler

Dry ballpoint pen

Rag stock paper

Decorative accent, as desired (embossed stamped image, dried and pressed leaf or small flower, charm, bead, postage stamp, sticker, etc.)

1. Use ruler and dry ballpoint pen to mark four points that define a 10-inch-by-7-inch rectangle on rag stock.

2. To deckle edge, lay ruler along two points that mark one side, pressing down firmly on ruler with hand. Use opposite hand to fold side of paper up against ruler to make crease. Tear paper against edge of ruler, allowing a rough "deckle" to form. Repeat with remaining sides. Fold paper in half crosswise to create center crease in 5-inch-by-7-inch card. Open card flat in horizontal position right side up.

3. Use ruler and dry ballpoint pen to mark four points that define a 1½-inch square on top third of right panel, leaving a 1-inch border to the right and top of the square. To deboss line, run dry ballpoint pen firmly along edge of ruler, pressing to indent line. Repeat for remaining three sides of square. If desired, add second debossed square within first as shown.

4. Decorate center square with chosen stamped image, or as desired.

Elegant Note Card | *finished size: 5″ x 5″*

Forget plain white copy paper. You can use a copy machine to print exquisite line art on clear overlay film and pair it with elegant paper in soft pastels. This combination maximizes modern technology without sacrificing the elegant look and sophistication of traditional note cards.

1. On self-healing mat, measure, mark, and cut one 10-inch-by-5-inch rectangle from medium-weight paper, using ruler, pencil, and X-Acto knife.

2. Fold rectangle in half crosswise, then open flat in horizontal position, wrong side facing up.

3. On center of left panel, measure, mark, and cut a 2-inch square, using ruler, pencil, and X-Acto knife. Note: Window is marked and cut on interior of card to avoid marring front right panel, which is display side.

4. Read instructions on package of clear overlay film, then take card, art, and overlay film to copy store.

5. Copy line art on plain white paper, enlarging or reducing image as necessary, so that it fits inside cutout window.

6. Hand feed overlay film into top paper tray of copier as directed by manufacturer's instructions, and lay sized art, image side down, on top of glass. Print art on film, allowing ink to dry completely.

7. Center film image over cutout window and trim film so that it measures 3 inches square.

8. Open card flat, wrong side up.

9. Lay film image over cutout window, using short lengths of double-stick tape to secure.

In the Doghouse | *finished size: 4" x 4"*

Cut a doghouse puzzle from glossy papers in jewel tones and accent it with a brass charm. This project is so fast and fabulous you will want to make smaller versions and use them as place setting cards or small gift cards for packages.

YOU WILL NEED:

Self-healing mat

Cardstock in white

Straightedge ruler

#1 pencil

X-Acto knife

Pattern (page 105)

Tracing paper

Low-tack masking tape

Cardstock with matte finish in lavender,
    mint green, and yellow

Dry ballpoint pen

Glue stick

1. On self-healing mat, measure, mark, and cut one 8-inch-by-5-inch rectangle from white cardstock, using ruler, pencil, and X-Acto knife.

2. Fold rectangle in half crosswise. Set aside.

3. Using pencil and ruler, trace roof, house, and background sections of the pattern on tracing paper. You may want to secure tracing paper to the page with masking tape to prevent slipping.

4. Lay lavender cardstock wrong side up on self-healing mat.

5. Lay tracing paper pattern, wrong side up, on lavender cardstock and use pen to trace along marked line of the roof only, pressing down firmly to transfer lines. (See Jeweled Butterfly, page 22, step 2.) Set aside.

6. Repeat steps 3 and 4 to mark the house section only on wrong side of mint green cardstock, and the background section only on wrong side of yellow cardstock.

7. On self-healing mat, cut out roof, house, and background sections, using X-Acto knife and ruler.

8. Use glue stick to attach each section to front panel of white card.

Sticker Postcard | *finished size: 5" x 7"*

A great shortcut to making custom-designed stickers is to use a copier. By arranging a collection of favorite images on plain paper and copying them onto self-adhesive paper that is made for a copier, you can create an entire sheet of personalized stickers for just pennies. Color them if you want to. Then, cut them out and use them to decorate your cards.

YOU WILL NEED:

Self-healing mat

Cardstock in pastel color with semi-gloss finish

Straightedge ruler

Pencil

X-Acto knife

Copyright-free art: full-color illustrations in holiday motifs or as desired (e.g., vintage labels, maps, photographs)

Manicure scissors

Glue stick

Self-adhesive white paper

Colored markers, pencils, or watercolors with paintbrush (optional)

Note: You will need access to a photocopy machine.

1. On self-healing mat, cut a 7-inch-by-5-inch rectangle from cardstock, using ruler, pencil, and X-Acto knife. Set aside.

2. Bring chosen art to copy store.

3. Copy selected single images on plain white paper, using a black-and-white copy machine.

4. Select and use manicure scissors to cut out favorite motifs, ganging them on an 8½-inch-by-11-inch sheet of copy paper, using glue stick to affix them.

5. Lay sheet of paste-up of motifs on top of glass of copy machine, face down, then lay self-adhesive paper in top paper tray, following manufacturer's directions.

6. Print, and allow ink on copy to dry completely.

7. If desired, hand color motifs, using markers, pencils, or watercolors.

8. Use scissors to cut around motif, then peel off sticker and press to front of card in position, as desired.

Three Little Windows | *finished size: 4½" x 8"*

A contemporary pamphlet-style design with earnest lines lights up when it is made with papers in attention-getting colors. The fun cover with the cutout windows allows for some good-natured mischief. Inscribe three interesting words inside the small windows, then tell the dish inside on the tiered levels of paper.

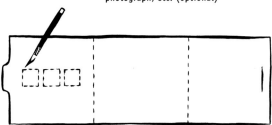

1. On self-healing mat, measure, mark, and cut a 4½-inch-by-16½-inch rectangle from cardstock using ruler, pencil, and X-Acto knife.

2. Fold bottom end up to create a 4-inch flap. Fold top end down to create a 4½-inch flap. Ends will overlap.

3. Open card flat, wrong side up. Mark midpoint of top and bottom sides, using pencil. Mark two points on top edge, each ¼ inch from marked midpoint. Mark and cut away a ¼-inch strip along the top edge, stopping at the two outside marks, leaving the paper in between the marks uncut. To finish tab, neatly snip away narrow strips at either side of tab, using scissors.

4. Fold bottom flap up and top flap down so that tab overlaps bottom flap. Mark position of tab on bottom flap, using pencil, then open card and cut a vertical slit, using X-Acto knife, in bottom flap so that tab slips in easily when card is closed.

5. Open card flat, then measure, mark, and cut a row of three ½-inch-square windows in top panel, following diagram, using ruler and X-Acto knife.

6. Measure, mark, and cut two 4½-inch-by-8-inch sheets of each color stationery.

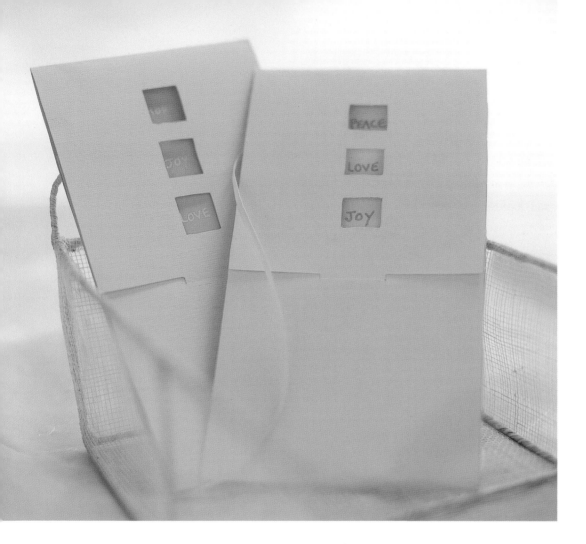

7. Slip blue pages into card and close card. Using pencil, lightly mark blue paper at the top side of the center square. Remove pages.

8. On self-healing mat, trim away top edge of blue pages ¼ inch above the pencil mark, using ruler and X-Acto knife.

9. Repeat step 7 using pink paper and marking the paper at the top side of bottom square. Repeat step 8, trimming away top edge ¼ inch above pencil mark.

10. Position green pages in card, followed by blue pages and pink pages, using cement to secure bottom edge of papers to each other and to cover.

11. Fold over flaps and insert tab in slit.

12. Inscribe a letter or short word on stationery inside window; or glue bead, button, or tiny photograph in each pane.

Wallpaper | *finished size: 6" x 6"*

You can print sophisticated cards in seconds. To create a dramatic note card, rubber stamp an image in one color on cardstock in a contrasting color. Then emboss the image to a high shine using embossing powder and a heat gun.

YOU WILL NEED:

Self-healing mat

Medium-weight matte paper in cream

Pencil

Straightedge ruler

X-Acto knife

Large wall stamp

Gold stamp pad

Gold embossing powder

Soft-bristle paintbrush

Heat gun

Ribbon

1. On self-healing mat, measure, mark, and cut a 12-inch-by-12-inch square from medium-weight matte paper using pencil, ruler, and X-Acto knife.

2. Lay matte paper flat on work surface and fold card in half horizontally, bringing top edges to meet bottom edges. Fold card in half again, bringing left edges to meet right edges. Open card up and lay flat on work surface so front of card is on the right.

3. Press wall stamp onto ink pad so that rubber surface is completely covered. Center image, ink side down, on front of card, pressing to transfer motif. Sprinkle embossing powder over stamped image, shaking paper to remove excess powder and using soft brush to remove any stray particles. Place heat gun over stamped area until embossing powder melts.

4. Fold card. Lay a ribbon in center fold like a bookmark.

e n v e l o p e s

Gatefold Envelope

The gatefold envelope creates an air of fantasy by virtue of the "gates" that turn back like the doors of a cupboard. When opened, the slender panels reveal the whole card at once, creating immediate drama and impact. This envelope, like the Square and Standard envelopes, can be adapted to fit any card.

YOU WILL NEED:

Cardstock

Pencil

Straightedge ruler

Self-healing mat

X-Acto knife

Self-adhesive seal or sticker

1. Place card vertically on cardstock that is wrong side up and trace around edges, using pencil.

2. Measure and mark a rectangle or square $^3/_8$ inch larger than the size of the card, using ruler and pencil. Use this new, larger rectangle or square to guide all other measurements. Measure and mark rectangles half the width but equal the length of the center rectangle on both left and right sides, using ruler and pencil. Measure and mark $^1/_2$ inch from top and bottom edges, using ruler and pencil. See diagram.

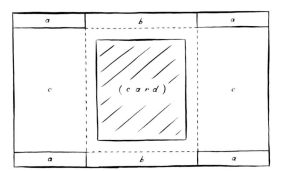

3. On self-healing mat, cut around outer edge, using X-Acto knife.

4. On self-healing mat, cut away all four A sections using X-Acto knife. Lay rectangle vertically, wrong side up. Fold in B sections at designated lines. Fold in C sections at designated lines.

5. Fold back B sections to slip in card and fold them in again, followed by C sections.

6. Use self-adhesive seal or sticker to keep card closed.

Square Envelope

Square shaped cards that are graphically uncluttered tend to work well with the straightforward shape and style of the square envelope. Square envelopes can carry cards that have a formal or informal air and can be made in coordinating papers that create an appealing harmony of design elements.

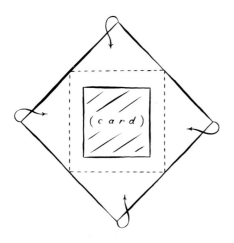

1. Place card on cardstock that is wrong side up and trace around edges, using pencil.

2. Measure and mark a square $^3/_8$ inch larger than the size of the card, using ruler and pencil. Use this new, larger square to guide all other measurements.

3. On self-healing mat, measure, mark, and cut a larger square, following pattern, using ruler, pencil, and X-Acto knife. Fold all four corners toward center. See diagram.

4. Unfold and slip in card.

5. Fold envelope back up and close, using a self-adhesive seal or sticker.

Standard Envelope

The standard envelope is a dependable style for most cards since it is so easy to make. Comprised of flaps that fold up neatly, the standard envelope is like a form-fitting pocket into which you can slip a card of any size, whether sturdy square or sleek rectangle.

YOU WILL NEED:

Medium-weight paper

Pencil

Straightedge ruler

Self-healing mat

X-Acto knife

Rubber cement

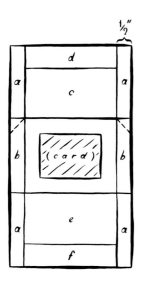

1. Place card on medium-weight paper that is wrong side up and trace around edges, using pencil.

2. Measure and mark a rectangle or square $^3/_8$ inch larger than the size of the card, using ruler and pencil. Use this new, larger rectangle or square to guide all other measurements. Measure and mark a second rectangle or square of equal size below the first, using ruler and pencil. Measure and mark a third rectangle or square above the first. Measure and mark $^1/_2$ inch from right and left edges, using ruler and pencil. See diagram.

3. On self-healing mat, cut around outer edge, using X-Acto knife.

4. On self-healing mat, cut away all four A sections and cut angle on top of B sections, using X-Acto knife. Lay rectangle vertically, wrong side up. Fold inward at all designated lines, then smooth flat again. Fold in B sections. Fold down section D onto section C and adhere using rubber cement. Fold in sections F and E. Place a thin layer of rubber cement ($^1/_2$ inch wide) on right and left outside edges of section E. Fold section E toward B sections, creating a pocket; press down to adhere. Fold down section C to complete envelope.

5. Place card inside envelope; use rubber cement to seal.

Technical Glossary | *Glossary of Terms*

The following words and terms are defined according to *Merriam Webster's Collegiate Dictionary*, 10th *Edition*, and are interpreted according to the scope of the work. For more information on any of the following, consult larger references dedicated to the subject.

beading needle: a long, thin needle designed specifically to thread and sew small (1mm) beads.

calligraphy pen: a hand-held writing implement with a broad nib that depends on direction, slant, and pressure to form letters and numerals characterized by thick and thin lines.

cardstock: flat, stiff, heavyweight paper that provides structure to card formats that require support; often cut and folded to make outside cards and envelopes.

charcoal paper: lightweight paper that has low relief texture, characterized by striations.

chipboard: flat, stiff, one-, two-, and three-ply cardboard used to reinforce or provide structure to lightweight paper.

clear overlay film: flat, transparent, glossy acetate that takes images printed by a photocopy machine.

composition gold leaf: also called Dutch metal; a metal alloy that comes in thin 5-inch-square sheets, used to gild surfaces; usually adhered using size when applied to nonporous surfaces and can be applied to porous surfaces using rubber cement.

contact cement: a thick, amber-colored mucilage that creates a strong and permanent bond between two materials; applied in dry-mount technique where surfaces are coated with cement, allowed to dry, and then pressed together to create a strong bond. It is generally nontoxic, although it needs to be used in a well-ventilated room.

corrugated paper: textured two-ply paper with a rippled surface; the trough section of ripple is often glued to lightweight backing paper, which prevents crimping. It needs to be scored to create a straight fold.

darning needle: a thick needle with a large eye, often used to sew with yarn; available in varying lengths in blunt and sharp points.

deboss: to indent a surface using a rounded instrument like a stylus or dry ballpoint pen.

deckle: a process of creating an uneven, feathery edge along the side of heavyweight paper; edge is caused by a frame used in making handmade paper. The effect can be most successfully reproduced on rag stock using a tear technique.

decoupage: the art of decorating surfaces with cutout pieces of paper that are glued down and coated with decoupage glue, and then protected with several layers of varnish.

decoupage glue: a viscous translucent adhesive used to apply paper images using decoupage.

dossier: a file containing detailed information about a person or subject.

dry-mount: a method by which materials are joined using pressure or contact between two materials that have been coated with rubber cement, contact cement, or spray adhesive. The method requires that each surface be coated with a light application of adhesive that is then allowed to dry, after which materials are pressed together for a tight bond. It is used to bond two sheets of paper without wrinkling; materials dry-mounted with rubber cement can be peeled apart and repositioned once after the first mount. The disadvantage of rubber cement as a dry-

mount adhesive is that it is applied with a brush, which does not coat evenly and which is impractical on large surfaces. Contact cement bonds heavier materials better than rubber cement.

emboss: to raise in relief a line or portion of paper by scoring or by applying inks that build up the surface with melted particles where applied; popularly used as a decorative treatment using rubber stamps, ink, glitter, and a heat gun.

embossing powder: a grainy material made from tiny particles of either metal or plastic, bound together by a heating process in which particles melt and adhere to paper or other porous material. All embossing powder will become permanent when melted, even the grains that may stick on paper.

ephemera: collectibles usually made of paper, either printed or cut; can be any mementos, such as ticket stubs, trinkets, ribbon, and the like, that have decorative but little intrinsic dollar value.

fabric glue: like high-tack white glue; a nontoxic glue that adheres fabric to other materials without staining and air dries at a medium rate.

fabric markers: permanent markers that will not bleed or wash away when used on fabric.

folio: sheets of paper folded once and inserted in a slip case, creating the "pages" of a book; often held together at the fold using thread, ribbon, twine, or staples.

gatefold: a folded card that opens out from the middle, as a gate would, as opposed to from the side.

glossy stock: paper with a smooth, shiny surface that is sensitive to grease, dirt, and scratching; should be protected with plain paper while being handled.

heat gun: a hand-held heat dispenser that emanates focused heat so that it can be used to melt embossing powder.

high-tack white glue: a thick nontoxic white adhesive with a pasty consistency that is used to join porous materials; dries at faster rate than white glue and usually does not warp paper unless applied in thick coats.

hot-glue gun: a hand-held glue dispenser that heats glue sticks and dispenses melted glue through the nozzle.

kraft paper: industrial paper made from wood pulp and resembling brown paper bags; available in three weights: light, medium, and heavy.

low-tack masking tape: paper tape that secures the position of one section of a sheet of paper to another; can be removed easily without damaging the paper.

matte: a dull finish, lacking luster or gloss.

micro-glitter: glitter made from tiny particles that melt when exposed to heat.

muslin: a plain, woven, sheer to coarse cotton fabric; can be natural or bleached.

organza: lightweight, often sheer fabric made from silk, rayon, or nylon thread; resembles organdy.

paint chips: paper strips coated with paint made by paint manufacturers so clients can assess color choices.

paper: flat material made from wood pulp and processed into sheets.

LIGHTWEIGHT: sheer, translucent, or opaque paper often used as an overlay (tracing vellum, gift wrap, parchment, rice, tissue, or charcoal; or writing stationery with linen).

MEDIUM-WEIGHT: paper with a glossy-coated, faux-style texture (suede,

leather or snakeskin, 1-ply chipboard or bristol); bends slightly when stood on end.

HEAVYWEIGHT OR CARDSTOCK: a stiff-structured paper that does not bend when stood on end (100% rag, 65-lb. watercolor, 2-ply chipboard or mat board).

photo transfer: adhesive-backed photo-sensitive paper used to print on T-shirts and papers with a high rag content.

press type: self-adhesive letters and numerals, usually made from pliable vinyl.

rag stock: paper made from 100% cotton rags; has a soft, fine hand with a smooth or slightly textured surface, ideal for making cards with a deckle edge using a tear technique.

rotary cutter: a single-handled cutting implement with a wheel-shaped blade; excellent for making clean, straight cuts in fabric, suede, and fine papers.

rubber cement: an adhesive with plasticity made especially for use on paper due to its nonwrinkling and noncurling properties.

saddle stitch: a style of decorative stitching created by setting a sewing machine to baste so that long stitches are visible; can be done by hand.

score: a very narrow groove in paper made by running a stylus or dry ballpoint pen against a straightedge ruler using pressure; used to make folds neat. Paper folds away from a scored mark.

seed beads: 1-mm beads made from clear glass or plastic.

self-adhesive: paper or Mylar with adhesive backing that adheres on contact.

self-healing mat: a cutting surface made from dense rubber whose cuts close after a blade is passed over the surface, so as to maintain a smooth cutting surface.

spray adhesive: rubber cement dispensed from an aerosol can; excellent for laminating two light- to medium-weight papers and fabrics. It needs to be used in a well-ventilated room.

steel-etched engravings: fine-line drawings made by scratching the surface of a metal plate with a stylus so that the image is printed when the plate is coated with ink and paper is laid on the etching.

stencil: a pattern formed by cutting a shape and printing from the negative space left by the cutout.

tear technique: the process of creating a deckle-style edge associated with hand-made paper. Rag stock is folded against the edge of a metal ruler, then lifted and torn against the metal edge, tearing and exposing threads in an attractive, uneven pattern associated with expensive hand-made papers.

template: a form or pattern used to guide the drafting of a shape.

"T"-pin: a steel pin with a sharp point at one end and a crossbar at the opposite end, used to make starter holes for beading with a needle too weak to puncture paper without breaking.

tracing paper: lightweight translucent paper used to mark the lines of a pattern.

variegated ribbon: fabric ribbon in varying shades of one or more colors made by changing the value and shade of the dye.

Velcro: a two-part closure of identical shapes, consisting of one section with small hooks that sticks to a corresponding section with small loops.

vellum: a lightweight translucent paper that appears frosted; often used as an overlay, and available in three weights: light, medium, and heavy.

wire-edge ribbon: ribbon with thin copper wire sewn into its edges that allows it to have "memory," so that the ribbon keeps its shape when manipulated.

X-Acto knife: originally a manufacturer's name and now a common name for a utility knife that has an angled metal blade attached to a cylindrical handle; used for cutting clean lines. Blades are available in several styles and thicknesses and are made to be replaced, thereby guaranteeing clean cuts.

Patterns

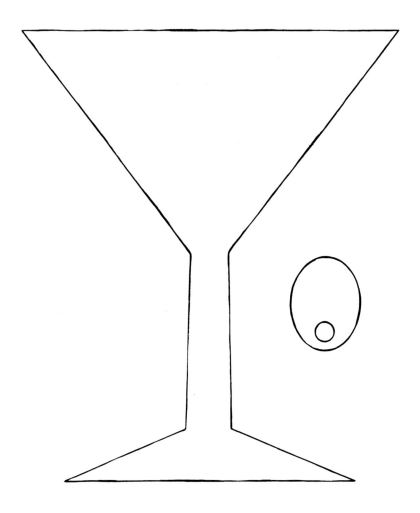

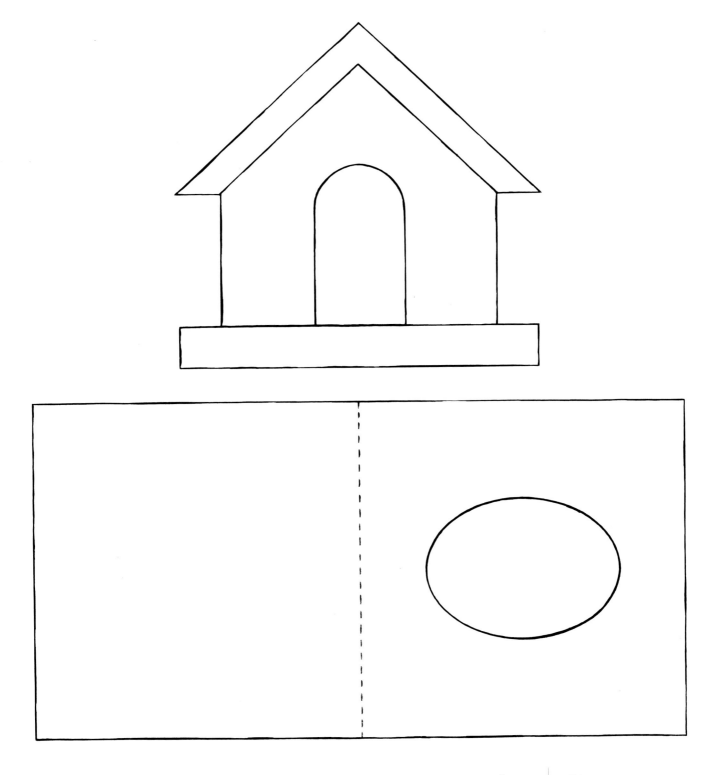

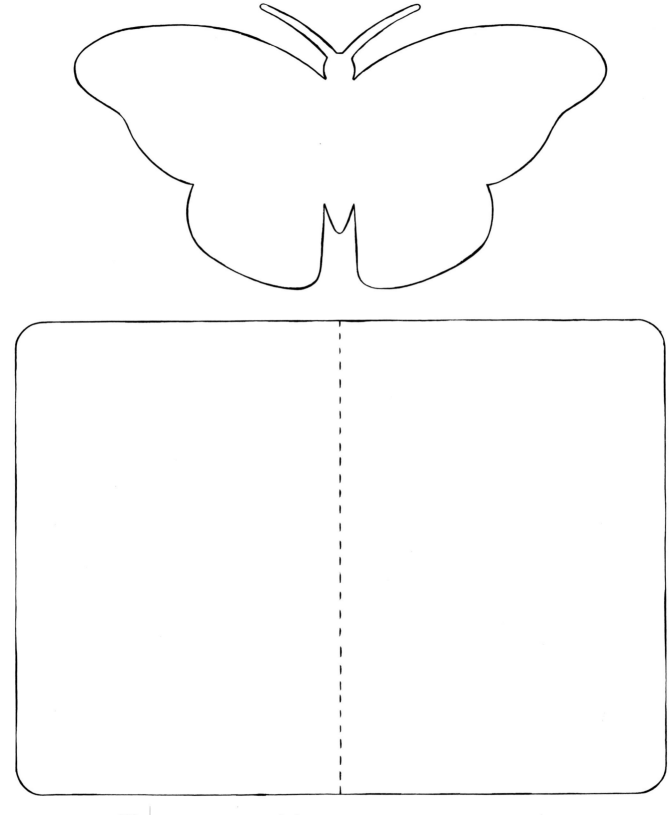

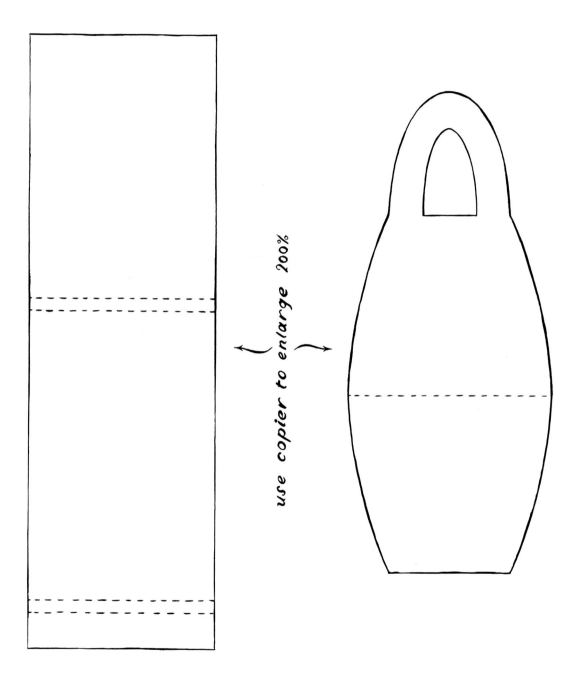

use copier to enlarge 200%

index

All That Glitters, 76
Anniversary Dossier, 39

baby, new
    Miniature Baby Album, 14-15
    Peas in a Pod, 16
    The Royal Addition, 12-13
birthdays. *See also* baby, new
    Classic Art, 18
    Flirty Purse, 21
    Jeweled Butterfly, 22
    Sweet 16, 24-25
Bread-and-Butter Notes, 44-45
Brighter than the Best, 59
Butterfly, Jeweled, 22

Center of Attention, 86
Christmas
    All That Glitters, 76
    Christmas Tree, 70
    Coupon Gift Book, 74-75
    Paper Lantern, 68-69
Classic Art, 18
Country Sachet, 47
Coupon Gift Book, 74-75

Doghouse, In the, 90

Easter, 81
Egg in the Window, 81
Elegant Note Card, 88-89
envelopes
    Gatefold Envelope, 99
    Square Envelope, 100
    Standard Envelope, 101

Festival of Lights, 72-73
Fiesta, 60
Flirty Purse, 21

Gatefold Envelope, 99
Gift Book, Coupon, 74-75

Hanukkah, 72-73

In the Doghouse, 90

Jeweled Butterfly, 22

Label, Vintage, 40
Love Knot, 36

love letters. *See also* weddings
    Anniversary Dossier, 39
    Love on the Rocks, 30
    Matchbox Valentine, 32-33
    Ransom Note, 29
    Vintage Label, 40

Matchbox Valentine, 32-33
Memory Book, 82
Miniature Baby Album, 14-15
Missing Your Easy Company, 48

New Year's Eve, 78-79

On the Road, 62

Paper Lantern, 68-69
Passport, 65
Peas in a Pod, 16
Purse, Flirty, 21

Ransom Note, 29
A Room with a View, 56
The Royal Addition, 12-13

Sachet, Country, 47
Shaken, Not Stirred, 78-79
Square Envelope, 100
Standard Envelope, 101
Stay in Touch, 50-51
Sticker Postcard, 93
Sweet 16, 24-25

Tassel and Tie, 33
Three Little Windows, 94-95
travel
    Fiesta, 60
    On the Road, 62
    Passport, 65
    A Room with a View, 56

Valentine, Matchbox, 32-33
Vintage Label, 40

Wallpaper, 96
weddings
    Love Knot, 36
    Wedding Masterpiece, 34
Welcome Home, 53
work, 59